COOL CASTLES AND PALACES
EDINBURGH CASTLE

by Clara Bennington

pogo

Ideas for Parents and Teachers

Pogo Books let children practice reading informational text while introducing them to nonfiction features such as headings, labels, sidebars, maps, and diagrams, as well as a table of contents, glossary, and index.

Carefully leveled text with a strong photo match offers early fluent readers the support they need to succeed.

Before Reading

• "Walk" through the book and point out the various nonfiction features. Ask the student what purpose each feature serves.

• Look at the glossary together. Read and discuss the words.

Read the Book

• Have the child read the book independently.

• Invite him or her to list questions that arise from reading.

After Reading

• Discuss the child's questions. Talk about how he or she might find answers to those questions.

• Prompt the child to think more. Ask: What did you know about Edinburgh Castle before you read this book? What more would you like to learn about it?

Pogo Books are published by Jump!
5357 Penn Avenue South
Minneapolis, MN 55419
www.jumplibrary.com

Library of Congress Cataloging-in-Publication Data

Names: Bennington, Clara, author.
Title: Edinburgh Castle / by Clara Bennington.
Description: Pogo books edition.
Minneapolis, MN: Jump!, Inc., [2020]
Series: Cool castles and palaces
Includes index. | Audience: Ages 7-10.
Identifiers: LCCN 2018057566 (print)
LCCN 2018057712 (ebook)
ISBN 9781641288644 (ebook)
ISBN 9781641288637 (hardcover : alk. paper)
Subjects: LCSH: Edinburgh Castle (Edinburgh, Scotland)
Juvenile literature. | Edinburgh (Scotland)
Buildings, structures, etc.–Juvenile literature.
Castles–Scotland–Edinburgh–History–Juvenile literature.
Classification: LCC DA890.E4 (ebook)
LCC DA890.E4 E353 2020 (print) | DDC 941.3/4–dc23
LC record available at https://lccn.loc.gov/2018057566

Editor: Jenna Trnka
Designer: Molly Ballanger

Photo Credits: Madrugada Verde/Shutterstock, cover; Stefano_Valeri/Shutterstock, 1; Gaid Kornsilapa/Shutterstock, 3; bukki88/iStock, 4; AA World Travel Library/Alamy, 5; Angus McComiskey/Alamy, 6-7; Christophe Cappello/Shutterstock, 8-9; Scottish Viewpoint/Alamy, 10; Dylan Garcia Photography/Alamy, 11; simonbradfield/iStock, 12-13; Karol Kozlowski/age fotostock/SuperStock, 14-15; Kumar Sriskandan/Alamy, 16-17; Wikimedia, 18; anastas_styles/Shutterstock, 19; Gimas/Shutterstock, 20-21; Kate Connes/Shutterstock, 23.

Printed in the United States of America at Corporate Graphics in North Mankato, Minnesota.

TABLE OF CONTENTS

UPPER WARD

ST MARGARETS CHAPEL

DAVID'S TOWER

HALF MOON BATTERY & CASTLE WELL

CROWN SQUARE

TOILETS

LANG STAIRS & WAY OUT

26.99

CHAPTER 1

DEFENSIVE FORTRESS

Atop an extinct volcano in Edinburgh, Scotland, sits a **fortress**. It is more than 600 years old. This is Edinburgh Castle. It was built on Castle Rock to **defend** and protect.

Castle Rock

Enemies could be seen from miles away. Look out for Mons Meg! It is a giant **cannon**. It shot hefty cannon balls. Each weighed 400 pounds (180 kilograms)!

Mons Meg

cannon ball

PLEASE DO NOT CLIMB ON MONS MEG

drawbridge

Three **moats** once surrounded the castle. A drawbridge crossed them. It could be raised to keep attackers out.

If they did get across, Lang Stairs was the only way inside the castle. The flight of stairs was narrow and steep. Attackers had a hard time climbing up!

This is the Argyle **Battery**. Cannons face out. Parts of the wall are high. Why? They protected soldiers.

The castle was well protected. But control of it shifted many times. Why? Scotland and England fought to rule the country. Now they are both part of the United Kingdom.

DID YOU KNOW?

Every day at 1 pm, a loud cannon is fired. The **tradition** started in 1861! Why? It used to let ships nearby know what time it was.

CHAPTER 2

ROYAL RESIDENCE

Scottish **royalty** used to live in the castle. The crown jewels are still here. These are also known as the Honours of Scotland. They were used at the **coronation** of Mary, Queen of Scots in 1542.

Honours of Scotland

St. Margaret's **Chapel** is the oldest building in Edinburgh. It was built by King David I around 1130. The royal family used it. Baptisms, weddings, and funerals took place here.

St. Margaret's Chapel

Royals needed big rooms for feasts and **ceremonies**. The Great Hall was completed in 1511. A little window by the fireplace is called Laird's Lug. King James IV sometimes hid behind it. Why? He wanted to hear what people said about him!

Laird's
Lug

coat of
arms

IACOBVS PRIMVS BRITANNIAE
FRANCIAE ET HYBERNIAE REX

Laich Hall was used to host less important people. You can see the **coats of arms** of some of Scotland's kings and queens here.

WHAT DO YOU THINK?

Coats of arms are designs that identify noble families or people. If your family had a coat of arms, what would be on it? Why?

Royal Birthing Room

The Royal Birthing Room is where King James VI was born. It is a very tiny room. His mother, Mary, Queen of Scots, wanted a small, safe room for his birth. She was worried about enemies harming her baby.

TAKE A LOOK!

This map shows where some of the important places in the castle are. Take a look!

1 entrance
2 Argyle Battery
3 St. Margaret's Chapel
4 Mons Meg

5 Honors of Scotland
6 Royal Apartments
7 Great Hall

CHAPTER 3

WARTIME PRISON

The castle also served as a prison. When? During the American Revolution (1775–1783). Some soldiers who fought Britain were prisoners here. Many were skilled **craftsmen**. They made crafts, like model ships.

model ship

Life was not as easy for prisoners later. They were chained. During the 1800s, castle soldiers were sent here, too. They got locked up for fighting or falling asleep on duty.

Today, a war **memorial** and museum is here. Visitors can learn about life in the castle. Would you like to visit?

WHAT DO YOU THINK?

J. K. Rowling wrote the *Harry Potter* series. She spent a lot of time in Edinburgh. This castle may have inspired Hogwarts. Do you think it looks similar?

QUICK FACTS & TOOLS

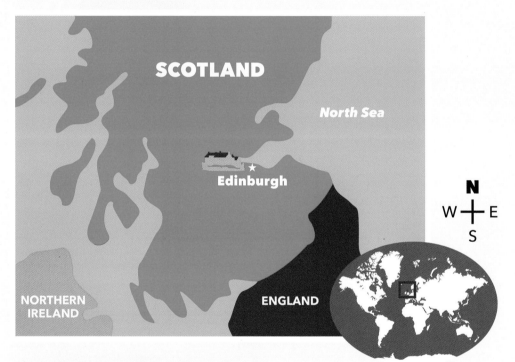

EDINBURGH CASTLE

Location: Edinburgh, Scotland

Year Construction Began (current castle): 1367

Size: 17,222 square feet (1,600 square meters)

Number of Rooms: 59

Current Residents: Members of military for castle protection

Average Number of Visitors Each Year: 1 million

battery: A grouping of artillery pieces used by soldiers.

cannon: A heavy gun, usually mounted on wheels, that fires large balls.

ceremonies: Formal events that mark important occasions.

chapel: A small church.

coats of arms: Designs on shields that identify noble families, people, cities, or organizations.

coronation: The ceremony of crowning a king or queen.

craftsmen: People who are skilled at making things with their hands.

defend: To protect from harm.

fortress: A place that is secured and protected against attack.

memorial: Something, such as a building, statue, or monument, that helps people remember a person or event.

moats: Deep, wide ditches dug around a castle and filled with water to prevent enemy attacks.

royalty: Kings, queens, and members of their families.

tradition: A custom, idea, or belief that is handed down from one generation to the next.

INDEX

TO LEARN MORE

Finding more information is as easy as 1, 2, 3.

❶ Go to www.factsurfer.com

❷ Enter "EdinburghCastle" into the search box.

❸ Choose your book to see a list of websites.

FACT SURFER